Second Edition

Impact
Listening

Ellen Kisslinger
Todd Beuckens

Series Editor
Michael Rost

1

PEARSON
Longman

Published by
Pearson Longman Asia ELT
20/F Cornwall House
Taikoo Place
979 King's Road
Quarry Bay
Hong Kong

The publisher's policy is to use **paper manufactured from sustainable forests**

fax: +852 2856 9578
email: pearsonlongman.hk@pearson.com
www.pearsonlongman.com

and Associated Companies throughout the world.

© Pearson Education Asia Limited 2007

This book was developed for Longman Asia ELT by Lateral Communications Limited.

First edition 2001
This edition 2007
Reprinted 2008 (three times)

Produced by Pearson Education Asia Limited, Hong Kong
SWTC/06

PROJECT DIRECTOR, SERIES EDITOR: Michael Rost
PROJECT COORDINATOR: Keiko Kimura
PROJECT EDITOR: Aaron Zachmeier
ART DIRECTOR: Inka Mulia
TEXTBOOK DESIGN: Inka Mulia
PRODUCTION COORDINATOR: Rachel Wilson
ILLUSTRATIONS: Ben Shanon, Violet Lemay
PHOTOGRAPHS: Bananastock, Blue Moon, Brand X Pictures, Dynamic Graphics, Iconotect, i dream stock, Image Source, Image Zoo, Inmagine, MIXA, Photodisc, Pixtal, Rubberball, Stockbyte, Tong Ro Image Photographers

AUDIO ENGINEER: Glenn Davidson
MUSIC: Music Bakery
TEST CONSULTANTS: Gary Buck, Natalie Chen
WEBSITE COORDINATOR: Keiko Kimura

IMPACT LISTENING 1
SB + CD   ISBN 978-962-00-5801-1
TM + Test CDs   ISBN 978-962-00-5804-2
Class CDs   ISBN 978-962-00-5807-3

IMPACT LISTENING 2
SB + CD   ISBN 978-962-00-5802-8
TM + Test CDs   ISBN 978-962-00-5805-9
Class CDs   ISBN 978-962-00-5808-0

IMPACT LISTENING 3
SB + CD   ISBN 978-962-00-5803-5
TM + Test CDs   ISBN 978-962-00-5806-6
Class CDs   ISBN 978-962-00-5809-7

Acknowledgements

The authors and editors would like to thank the many teachers and students who have used the *Impact Listening* series for their feedback. We also wish to thank the following people who contributed ideas, resources, stories, reviews and other feedback that helped us in the development of the second edition of the *Impact Listening* series:

Glenn Agius	Selana Allen	Kayra Arias
Sara Barrack	E. Biddlecombe	Jennifer Bixby
Eric Black	Erin Boorse	Christina Boyd
Rob Brezny	Jennie Brick	Karen Carrier
Richard Carter	Andrea Carvalho	Lydia Chen
Yen-yen Chen	Feodor Chin	Jeniffer Cowitz
Terry Cox	Kevin Davey	Payton Davis
Sandy Eriksen	Christine Feng	Andrew Finch
Masayoshi Fukui	Greg Gamaza	Mark Girimonte
Ann Gleason	Greg Gomina	Allison Gray
Marvin Greene	Scott Grinthal	Naomi Hagura
William Hayes	Patrick Heller	James Hobbs
Jessie Huang	Sarah Hunt	Caroline Hwang
Jason Jeffries	Wonchol Jung	Alex Kahn
An-Ran Kim	Ju Sook Kim	Akiko Kimura
Barbara Kucer	Norm Lambert	Elizabeth Lange
Ruth Larimer	Tae Lee	Wayne Lee
Jason Lewis	Li-chun Lu	Rami Margron
Amy McCormick	Alexander Murphy	Amy Murphy
Andre Nagel	Dalia Nassar	Petra Nemcova
Tim Odne	Jamie Olsen	Joy Osmanski
John Park	Jeremy Parsons	Jackie Pels
Jessica Raaum	Stacey Reeve	Kerry Rose
Amy Rubinate	Alicia Rydman	Elly Schottman
Jerome Schwab	Ellen Schwartz	Sam Shih
Sherry Shinn	Josh Snyder	Jim Swan
Craig Sweet	Donna Tatsuki	Steven Thomas
Nicke Toree	Steven Trost	Aurelie Vacheresse
Joanna Vaughn	Yao-yao Wei	Paul Weisser
J. J. White	Julie Winter	Johnny Wong
Carolyn Wu	Cesar Zepeda	

We also wish to thank our colleagues at Pearson Longman for their guidance and support during the development of the second edition of the series. In particular, we'd like to acknowledge (Hong Kong) Roy Gilbert, Christienne Blodget, Rachel Wilson, Tom Sweeney, Michael Chan, Eric Vogt, Vessela Gasper; (Japan) Shinsuke Ohno, Minoru Ikari, Jonah Glick, Takashi Hata, Yuji Toshinaga, Steve King, Masaharu Nakata, Donn Ogawa, Yuko Tomimasu, Mari Hirukawa, Hiroko Nagashima, Megumi Takemura, Alastair Lamond, Michiyo Mitamura, Ken Sasaki, Takeshi Kamimura, Meiko Naruse, Tomoko Ayuse, Kenji Sakai, Reiko Murota, Mayumi Abe, Minako Uta, Masako Yanagawa, Ayako Tomekawa, Katherine Mackay, Keiko Sugiyama; (Korea) Yong Jin Oh, Chong Dae Chung, Jan Totty, Rilla Roessel, Katherine Ji, Hyuk Jin Kwon, Tae Youp Kim, Sang Ho Bae, Moon Jeong Lim; (Taiwan) Golden Hong, Louis Lin, Constance Mo, Vivian Wang, Sherrie Lin, Christine Huang, Joseph Chan, David Ger; (Thailand) Narerat Ancharepirat, Chris Allen, Unchalee Boonrakvanich, Udom Sathawara, Sura Suksingh;

Special thanks to Jason Lewis, Expedition 360, Maw-Maw's Cajun Kitchen, the rock band Pink, Tech Trek, Maxima Corporation Japan Ltd., Earthfoot Ecotours, Hardscratch Press, $RealMoney$ Enterprises®, Petra Nemcova and Warner Books for permission to use an extract from *Love Always, Petra* © 2005 Warner Books.

The *Impact Listening* series is an innovative set of learning materials that helps students develop listening skills for social, academic and business purposes.

The series has three levels:
Impact Listening 1 (for beginning level students)
Impact Listening 2 (for high-beginning and low-intermediate students)
Impact Listening 3 (for intermediate and high-intermediate students)

Impact Listening makes listening an active and enjoyable experience for students. While featuring an abundance of natural listening input and a variety of creative activities, *Impact Listening* leads students to become successful listeners through an effective **4-step process**:

Step 1: **Build word-based listening skills**	Warm Up

To be successful listeners, we have to hear words and phrases accurately. With the **Warm Up**, each unit begins by helping students understand high-frequency words and phrases. As students become confident in their ability to "catch" common words and phrases, they increase their capacity for listening to longer stretches of language.

This section introduces common words and phrases related to the unit theme. With its interactive format, **Warm Up** gets all students involved at the outset of the lesson.

Step 2: **Develop focusing strategies**	Listening Task

It is important to have a purpose when we listen. Setting a purpose allows the students to become active listeners. In **Listening Task**, students are given a variety of tasks to focus their attention. A short follow-up speaking activity allows students to express their own ideas. They develop active listening strategies: **Prepare**, **Guess**, and **Focus**.

The section is a set of **two linked tasks** based on short natural listening extracts. The **First Listening** task focuses on understanding the gist, while the **Second Listening** task focuses on details. Vivid illustrations and photographs help students focus on meaning.

Step 3:
Practice idea-based strategies

Real World Listening

Everyone experiences difficulties when listening to a second language. While they work on building effective word-based (bottom-up) listening skills, it is also important that students practice idea-based (top-down) listening strategies. In **Real World Listening**, students work on key listening strategies: **Ask**, **Respond**, and **Review**.

Based on natural, extended conversations, monologues, and stories, this section helps students develop active listening strategies: predicting, inferring, clarifying, making judgments and responding to the ideas in the extract.

Step 4:
Integrate what you have learned

Interaction Link

Connecting to the topic is a vital part of becoming a better listener. Throughout each unit, students are given the opportunity to develop curiosity, activate their knowledge, and express their ideas and opinions. **Interaction Link** helps students link listening and speaking.

Interaction Link is a lively interactive speaking and listening task. Students have the opportunity to review what they have learned in the unit and use interactive tasks to produce real communication.

Impact Listening also includes:

Self-Study pages

For use with the Self-Study CD (included in the back of every Student Book), the Self-Study page provides new tasks for the Real World Listening extract, to allow students to review at home. (Answer Key is provided.)

Teacher's Manual

Teachers are encouraged to utilize the Impact Listening Teacher's Manual. This manual contains teacher procedures, insightful language and culture notes, full scripts, answer keys, and expansion activities. The Teacher's Manual also includes a Test Master CD-ROM and instructions for creating and administering the tests.

Website

Teachers and students are welcome to use the Impact Listening series website for additional ideas and resources.
www.impactseries.com

4

Impact Listening will help you use listening strategies. Listening strategies are ways of thinking actively as you listen. Here are the main strategies you will practice in this course:

Prepare

- Preparing helps you listen better.
- Before you listen, look at the illustrations and photographs. Think about the ideas.
- Look over the vocabulary words.
- Try to predict what the speakers will say.

Ask

- Good listeners ask a lot of questions.
- While you listen, think of questions: What do you want to know?

Become an Active Listener

Guess

- Guessing can make you a more successful listener.
- Make your best guess at the parts you don't understand.

Respond

- Responding is part of listening!
- While you listen, pay attention to the speaker's ideas and intentions.
- After you listen, respond to the ideas: What do you think?

Focus

- Focus = Listen with a purpose.
- Before you listen, look at the listening task or questions.
- While you listen, focus on the task and questions. Listen for key words.
- If there are some words you don't understand, that's OK. Keep listening.

Review

- Reviewing builds your "listening memory."
- After you listen, think about the meaning of what the speakers have said.
- Try to say the meaning in your own words.

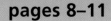

"How's it going?"

Warm Up

 Look at the pictures. Write the missing words.

what's	how	how's	long	I'm	nice

Jack: Hey, guys, _what's_ up?
Lucy: Oh, nothing much.

Hugh: Hi, Marci. _____ are
you doing?
Marci: Oh, you know. Pretty
good. How about you?

Suzie: Hi, Alan. _____ time
no see.
Alan: Hey, what a surprise.
Good to see you.

Tony: Hello, _____ Tony
Martin.
Claire: Oh, you're Tony. I'm
glad you're here.

Alex: Hi, Jeff. _____ it going?
Jeff: Not bad ... not bad at all.

Don: It's _____ to see
you again, Sue.
Sue: It's good to see you, too,
Don.

 Now listen and check.

CD 1, Track 2

How about you.
Hi! It's nice
to see you.

? USEFUL EXPRESSIONS
Hey, what's up?   *not much*
                    OK
Hi, how's it going?
It's been a long time.
Hello. It's good to see you again.
See you later.   *you, too!*

8

 Greet five classmates. Use different greetings.

Okay. Take   *I'll see you again*
it easy.   *soon.*

Listening Task

Look at the pictures. Where are the people?

First Listening: How do the people greet each other? Check (✔) the greeting.

CD 1, Tracks 3–9

Street,   *Store.*

1

☐ "What's happening?"
✔ "What's up?"

2

☐ "How are you?"
☐ "How are you doing?"

3

☐ "How are you doing?"
☐ "How are you today?"

4

☐ "Good morning."
☐ "Good afternoon."

5

☐ "Anybody home?"
☐ "Anybody here?"

6

☐ "Hello, I'm Rob Martin."
☐ "Hi, I'm Rob Martin."

Second Listening: What do they talk about? Check (✔) the answer.

CD 1, Tracks 3–9

1. ✔ work ☐ school

2. ☐ travel ☐ shopping

3. ☐ family ☐ school

4. ☐ work ☐ sports

5. ☐ pets ☐ travel

6. ☐ work ☐ weather

 Choose one of the conversations. Try it with your partner.

Real World Listening

PREPARE

 Tomas is a student. It's the first day of the semester. Tomas talks to three people. Who are they? Look at the pictures. Write your guesses in the boxes.

| his roommate | a professor | a classmate |
| a friend | his mother | his girlfriend |

Tomas

 Now listen and check.

CD 1, Tracks 10–13

GET THE MAIN IDEAS

What do they talk about? (There may be more than one correct answer.)

CD 1, Tracks 10–13

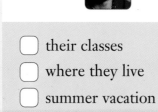

Part 1: Eddie	Part 2: Yuki	Part 3: Dr. Collins
☐ their classes	☐ their classes	☐ homework
☐ where they live	☐ their summer vacation	☐ a class
☐ summer vacation	☐ their teacher	☐ a schedule

RESPOND TO THE IDEAS

How does Tomas feel when he talks to Eddie, Yuki, and Dr. Collins? Why do you think so? Check (✔) the correct answers.

He meets Eddie	He meets Yuki	He meets Dr. Collins
☐ happy	☐ bored	☐ nervous
☐ sad	☐ excited	☐ angry

MEET YOUR CLASSMATES

1. Work alone. Match the questions with the squares below.

1. Do you live near here?
2. Do you have friends in class?
3. Is your shirt new?
4. Do you play sports?
5. Do you speak any other languages?
6. Is this your first English class?
7. Do you need English for your job?
8. Are you a good cook?

9. Do you listen to pop songs in English?
10. Do you watch TV in English?
11. Are you in any clubs?
12. Are you into the Internet?
13. Do you come from a big family?
14. Do you read in your free time?
15. Do you have a dog or cat?
16. Have you been overseas?

2. Ask your classmates and teacher questions about the topics below. Write the person's name and his or her answer in a square. Try to fill in every square.

class	languages	clothes	sports
Question: 6	Question:	Question:	Question:
Name:	Name:	Name:	Name:
Answer:	Answer:	Answer:	Answer:
TV	**job**	**music**	**home**
Question:	Question:	Question:	Question:
Name:	Name:	Name:	Name:
Answer:	Answer:	Answer:	Answer:
computers	**food**	**travel**	**friends**
Question:	Question:	Question:	Question:
Name:	Name:	Name:	Name:
Answer:	Answer:	Answer:	Answer:
hobby	**family**	**books**	**pets**
Question:	Question:	Question:	Question:
Name:	Name:	Name:	Name:
Answer:	Answer:	Answer:	Answer:

"It's a great place."

Warm Up

Match the pictures to the sentences.

1. __J__ I need a big **desk** for all my books.

2. ____ This **couch** is great. It's so comfortable.

3. ____ I love my **bed**. It's really soft.

4. ____ I love to soak in the **bathtub** after a long day.

5. ____ I need a new **lamp** in this room. It's very dark in here.

6. ____ Sit in this **chair** and relax.

7. ____ Here's my new **stove**. I love it.

8. ____ This **table** is too small for our family. There are six of us.

9. ____ Look at my new **poster**. Do you like it?

10. ____ Look out this **window**. It's a great view.

Now listen and check.

CD 1, Track 14

Ask your partner about his or her home.

12

USEFUL EXPRESSIONS

What's it like?
That's a good location.
How big is it?
It has ...
It's kind of ...

👁 **What kind of places do you think the people live in?**

🎧 **First Listening:** Do the people like their living situations? Check the correct answer.

CD 1, Tracks 15–19

1 Joe
2 Jason
3 Lisa
4 Steven

	Joe	Jason	Lisa	Steven
I really like it.	✔	☐	☐	☐
It's OK.	☐	☐	☐	☐
I don't like it.	☐	☐	☐	☐

🎧 **Second Listening:** Mark one thing they like (+) and one thing they don't like (–).

CD 1, Tracks 15–19

1
(+) The location.
(–) It's small.
☐ It's old.

2
☐ It's big.
☐ It's old.
☐ It's new.

3
☐ It's in a new building.
☐ It has big windows.
☐ It's on a busy street.

4
☐ It's in the mountains.
☐ It's far from the city.
☐ It's near the ocean.

Real World Listening

PREPARE

 Tim and Ronda are looking for a furnished apartment. Look at the two apartments below. Write the missing words.

Apartment 1

big _____   gas _____

king-size _____   on a busy _____

kitchen

balcony

stove

bathtub

bed

street

refrigerator

lake

Apartment 2

old _____   tiny _____

has a _____   near a _____

Now listen and check.

CD 1, Tracks 20–22

GET THE MAIN IDEAS

Check the correct information for each apartment.

CD 1, Tracks 20–22

Apartment 1				Apartment 2		
Rent	☐ $950	☐ $850 a month	**Location**	☐ good	☐ bad
Kitchen	☐ big	☐ small	**Rent**	☐ expensive	☐ reasonable
Appliances	☐ old	☐ new	**Size**	☐ big	☐ small
Bedrooms	☐ one	☐ two	**Furnished**	☐ yes	☐ no
Bed	☐ big	☐ small	**Bathroom**	☐ big	☐ small
Sofa	☐ new	☐ old	**Kitchen**	☐ big	☐ small
Floor	☐ wood	☐ carpet	**Appliances**	☐ old	☐ new
Location	☐ busy	☐ quiet	**Windows**	☐ a lot	☐ a few

RESPOND TO THE IDEAS

 Which apartment would you choose? Why?

14

A NEW PLACE TO LIVE

1. **You need a new place to live. What kind of place would you like? Look at the chart. What is more important to you? Check your preferences.**

	Me	Person A	Person B
Near a park	☐	☐	☐
Near a train station	☐	☐	☐
Old house (traditional)	☐	☐	☐
New apartment (modern)	☐	☐	☐
Family neighborhood (lots of children)	☐	☐	☐
Singles neighborhood (unmarried people)	☐	☐	☐
Quiet street (mostly homes)	☐	☐	☐
Busy street (lots of shops and nightlife)	☐	☐	☐
Nice view	☐	☐	☐
Big fence	☐	☐	☐
Old neighborhood (few new people)	☐	☐	☐
New neighborhood (lots of new people)	☐	☐	☐
Lots of light	☐	☐	☐
Big rooms	☐	☐	☐
Lots of new appliances	☐	☐	☐
Lots of antiques (old furniture)	☐	☐	☐
Big yard	☐	☐	☐
Small yard	☐	☐	☐
Bathtub only	☐	☐	☐
Shower only	☐	☐	☐
Furnished (comes with furniture but more expensive)	☐	☐	☐
Unfurnished (no furniture but a lot cheaper)	☐	☐	☐

2. **Now talk to two classmates. Find out what is important to them. Fill in the chart.**

3. **Now work with a new partner. Share the information in your charts. Together decide who is the better roommate for each of you, Person A or Person B.**

Warm Up

  Look at the people. What are they wearing? Unscramble the words.

 yellow

 green

 brown

 red

 orange

 blue

 purple

pink

gray

 black

1

ath
hat

2

wasthrites
sweatshirt

3

nassald
Sandals

4

anjes
Jeans

5

ghih shele
high heels

6

catjek
jacket

7

loop thirs
polo shirt

8

scalks
slacks

9

serds
dress

10

thrits
T shirt

11

aspamaj
Pajamas

12

tusi
suit

13

twaseer
sweater

14

groca spant
Cargo Pants

15

scosk
scoks
Socks

16

skanseer
sneakers

Now listen and check.

CD 1, Track 23

sweater

What are you wearing now?
Tell your partner.

USEFUL EXPRESSIONS
That looks great on you.
That's a good color for you.
Try a bigger/smaller size.
Is it me?
That's really nice.

Look at the pictures. What are the people shopping for?

*Check it out!
= look at this!*

First Listening: What suggestions do the people make? Check your answers.

CD 1, Tracks 24–30

1

- ☑ Try a different color.
- ☐ Try a different size.

2 *Sleeveless shirt*

- ☐ Try a smaller one.
- ☑ Try a bigger one.

3 *shoes.*

- ☐ Try a different size.
- ☑ Try a different color.

4 *tie suit*

- ☑ Try a different color.
- ☐ Try a different size.

5 *jeans*

- ☑ Try a bigger size.
- ☐ Try a smaller size.

6 *dress*

- ☐ Get a longer dress.
- ☑ Buy this one.

Second Listening: Check the comments you hear.

good on you

CD 1, Tracks 24–30

1.
- ☑ "Black looks good on you."
- ☐ "That looks good on you."

2.
- ☐ "That's really small."
- ☑ "That's a little small."

3.
- ☐ "I like these."
- ☑ "I like green."

4.
- ☐ "That's a good one."
- ☑ "That's a new one."

5.
- ☑ "Maybe a little too tight."
- ☐ "Maybe a little too loose."

6.
- ☐ "You look fantastic."
- ☑ "It looks good on you."

What clothes are popular now? What colors do you like to wear?

PREPARE

How do people want to look at a dance club? Check the words.

☑ sexy ☑ tall ☐ fun

☐ shy ☐ bored ☑ casual

☐ fancy ☑ cool ☐ trendy

Jenny is going to talk about what people wear at dance clubs. What do you think she wears?

Now listen and check.

CD 1, Tracks 31–32

GET THE MAIN IDEAS

Check the correct answers.

CD 1, Tracks 31–32

	Guys wear	Girls wear
T-shirts	☐	☐
Polo shirts	☐	☐
Cargo pants	☐	☐
Skirts	☐	☐
Jeans	☐	☐
Sneakers	☐	☐
High heels	☐	☐
Necklaces	☐	☐
Makeup	☐	☐
Perfume/cologne	☐	☐

RESPOND TO THE IDEAS

Do you like these clothes? What are your favorite clothes?

COOL OR WEIRD?

1. **Work alone. Look at the people. Which ones are "cool"? Which ones are "weird"? Why? Explain your opinions.**

☐1 ☐2 ☑3 ☐4 ☐5
cool   weird
Why?
_____

☐1 ☐2 ☐3 ☑4 ☐5
cool   weird
Why?
_____

☐1 ☐2 ☐3 ☐4 ☑5
cool   weird
Why?
_____

☐1 ☐2 ☐3 ☐4 ☐5
cool   weird
Why?
_____

☐1 ☐2 ☐3 ☐4 ☐5
cool   weird
Why?
_____

☐1 ☐2 ☐3 ☐4 ☐5
cool   weird
Why?
_____

2. **Form pairs. See if you agree or disagree about who is cool and who is weird. Give reasons.**

3. **Now compare your answers with another pair.**

"Where are you from?"

Togo

Warm Up

 Look at the map and write these countries in the boxes: Where do you think these students are from?

| Togo | Mexico | China | Iran | Russia | Japan | Spain | Greece |

| Luis | Tetsuya | Nick | Ana | Jiang Lee | Lalo |

Spain

| Hamid | Kojo |

 Now listen and check.

CD 1, Track 33

 Greet two classmates. Say where you are from. (If you are from the same country, say the city.)

USEFUL EXPRESSIONS

Where are you from?
Where is that?
I don't know where that is.
It's close to ...
I've always wanted to go there.

Listening Task

Look at the pictures. Some people are in the waiting room at an airport.
What do you think they are talking about?

First Listening: What nationality is the person?

CD 1, Tracks 34–39

1.
   - ☐ English
   - ☑ German

2.
   - ☐ Australian
   - ☐ British

3.
   - ☐ Spanish
   - ☐ Mexican

4.
   - ☐ Chinese
   - ☐ Japanese

5.
   - ☐ French
   - ☐ Canadian

Second Listening: What is the topic of each conversation?

CD 1, Tracks 34–39

1. ☐ a magazine
   ☑ a newspaper

2. ☐ Australian beaches
   ☐ British beaches

3. ☐ borrowing a phone
   ☐ buying something

4. ☐ a delayed flight
   ☐ a canceled flight

5. ☐ their flight
   ☐ speaking French

What things do you talk about when you first meet someone?

21

PREPARE

Rachel is visiting London. She meets some different people. Here are some parts of Rachel's conversations. Match the lines.

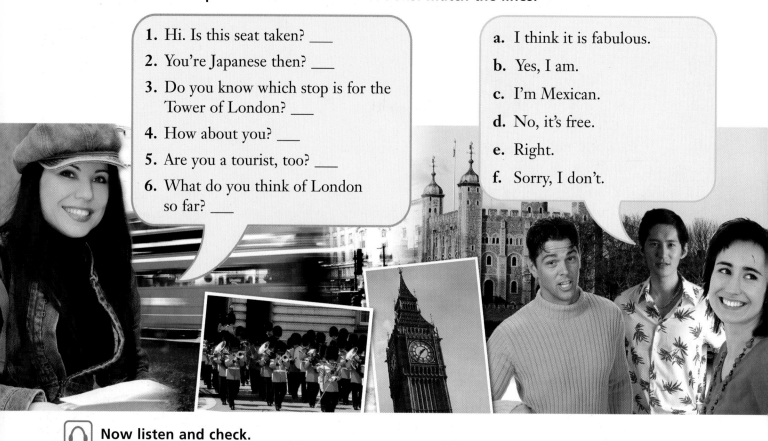

1. Hi. Is this seat taken? ___
2. You're Japanese then? ___
3. Do you know which stop is for the Tower of London? ___
4. How about you? ___
5. Are you a tourist, too? ___
6. What do you think of London so far? ___

a. I think it is fabulous.
b. Yes, I am.
c. I'm Mexican.
d. No, it's free.
e. Right.
f. Sorry, I don't.

Now listen and check.

CD 1, Tracks 40–43

GET THE MAIN IDEAS

Fill in the chart.

CD 1, Tracks 40–43

		is from	other information
Part 1	Hiro	Japan	He lived in _S F_. He loves _san fiong sxio_.
Part 2	Miguel	Mexican	He checks his _guidebook_. He thinks London is _great_.
Part 3	Silvia	France Italy	She drops her _map_. She is going to _visit tour London_. She thinks London is _fontti fbloz_.

RESPOND TO THE IDEAS

How can you describe each person? Use these words: _curious, friendly, warm, funny, helpful, quiet._

 Rachel is _____.

Hiro is _____.

 Miguel is _____.

 Silvia is _____.

WHERE'S IT FROM?

Work with a partner. Take turns talking about the words in the squares. Every time you can say where an item is from, you get the square. If you get five squares in a row, you win!

Napoleon	Bollywood	Panda	Petronas Towers	Kung Fu
France				
Surfing	BMW	Kangaroos	Machu Picchu	Lance Armstrong
Pizza	King Tut	MTV MUSIC TELEVISION ®	Jackie Chan	Great Barrier Reef
Yoga	Stonehenge	Samba	Eiffel Tower	Komodo Dragon
Tango	Kimchi	Maria Sharapova	Rap music	Tacos

"Do you know who that is?"

Warm Up

 Read the words and write them in the correct column.

chubby	thin	friendly	long
blond	curly	bald	funny
shy	outgoing	straight	tall
short	good-looking	brown	pretty

handsom = beautiful.

Body	Hair	Face	Personality
chubby			
tall	long	pretty	funny
chubby	blond	good-looking.	friendly
short	Brown		shy
good-looking			

 Now listen and check.

CD 1, Track 44

 Look at the people above. Describe a person to your partner. Can your partner guess who it is?

24

USEFUL EXPRESSIONS

Tell me about ...
She's a little chubby.
He has short brown hair.
She's really friendly.
He's fun to be with.

First Listening: Who are the people talking about? Write the names under the pictures.

CD 1, Tracks 45–49

1

Denise

2

sher tim

3

Kate

4

Jraht

 Second Listening: What are the people like? Write at least two things about each person.

CD 1, Tracks 45–49

1. tall, friendly, ...

2. scant intlient thery Cate

3. tonya guite intelingent blackhira

4. grand tall Cute veryCool

Ask your partner about a family member or a friend.

PREPARE

 Describe one of the people below. (Think about hair, face, body, clothes.)

GET THE MAIN IDEAS

Play People Bingo. Listen. Who are the people? Check the pictures. If you get three in a row, Bingo! (You win.)

CD 1, Tracks 50–51

PEOPLE BINGO!!!

RESPOND TO THE IDEAS

Play People Bingo with a partner.

CASTING CALL

Work with a partner. The two of you want to make a movie. There are three steps:
- decide what kind of movie you want to make
- decide what you want the actors to look like
- get a studio to agree to make the movie

1. **What kind of movie are you going to make? Check your choice.**

☐ Mystery	☐ Comedy	☐ Love story
☐ Action	☐ Animation	☐ Drama
☐ Horror	☐ Science fiction	☐ Documentary
☐ Sports	☐ Western	☐ Other

2. **What do you want the lead actors to look like? List the features for each actor, and then make a simple drawing.**

Lead Male Actor	Lead Female Actor
hair:	hair:
eyes:	eyes:
body type:	body type:
clothes:	clothes:
accessories:	accessories:
OVERALL LOOK	**OVERALL LOOK**

3. **Now work with another pair.**
   Pair one:
   - Visit the movie studio.
   - Present your actors and your movie idea.

   Pair two: (You work for the movie studio.)
   - Decide if you like the actors. Make suggestions for changes.
   - Decide if you want to make the movie.

"*What a nice family.*"

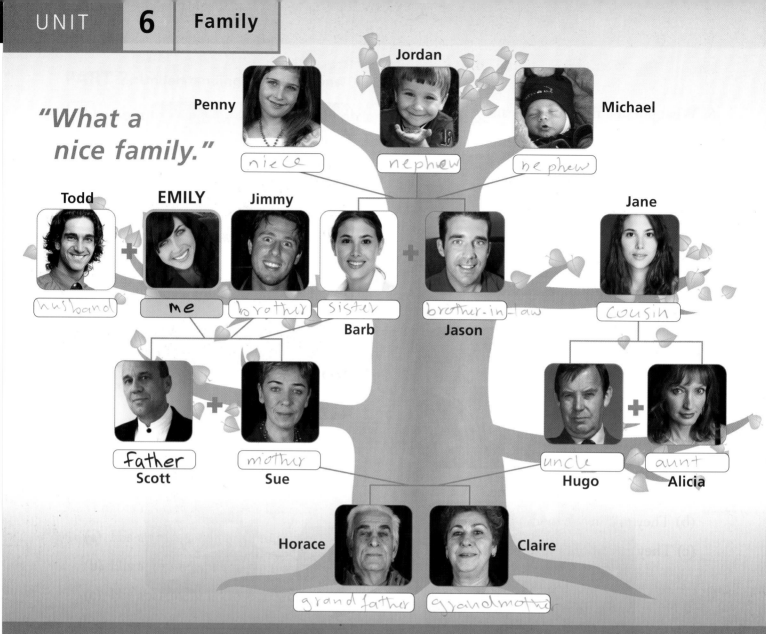

Jordan

Penny — niece

nephew

Michael — nephew

Todd — husband

EMILY — me

Jimmy — brother

Barb — sister

Jason — brother-in-law

Jane — cousin

Scott — father

Sue — mother

Hugo — uncle

Alicia — aunt

Horace — grandfather

Claire — grandmother

Warm Up

👁 Look at the family tree. How are the people related to Emily? Write the words in the family tree.

niece	husband	cousin
father/dad	grandfather	uncle
sister	nephew	brother-in-law
aunt	grandmother	
brother	mother/mom	son

I don't have eny in-laws

🎧 Now listen and check.

CD 1, Track 63

Draw your own family tree and show it to a partner.

USEFUL EXPRESSIONS

We're really close.
We get along pretty well.
There are four people in my family.
There are five of us.
We live together.

Listening Task

These are all family pictures of Beth at different ages.
What does she look like in each picture?

First Listening: Number the pictures and write Beth's age.

CD 1, Tracks 64–70

3

__1__ Beth's age __9__

2

____ Beth's age __7__

__3__ Beth's age __21__

5

4

__5__ Beth's age __25__

__6__ Beth's age __26__

____ Beth's age (about) ____

Second Listening: Where are they? Check the correct answer.

CD 1, Tracks 64–70

1. ☑ in the bedroom
   ☐ in the living room

2. ☐ at school
   ☑ in their yard

3. ☐ at their house
   ☑ at their grandmother's house

4. ☐ at her college
   ☑ in their backyard

5. ☐ at their home
   ☑ at the church

6. ☐ at Tiffany's parents' house
   ☑ at Phil's parents' house

How did Beth change as she got older?
How have you changed as you've gotten older?

33

Real World Listening

PREPARE

Eva Stone is the host of a show called *World Encounters.* Today's show is about four families. Here are the countries Eva visited. Write the countries in the boxes.

عربي

Honduras   Australia   China   Nigeria

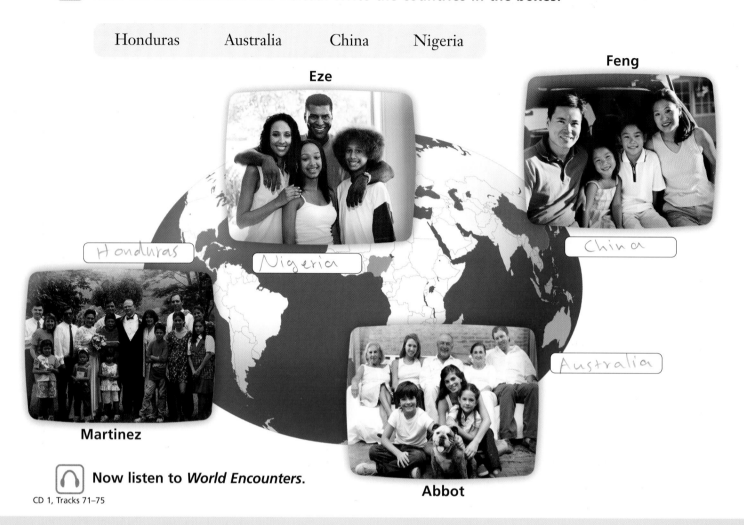

Eze

Feng

Honduras

Nigeria

China

Australia

Martinez

Abbot

 Now listen to *World Encounters.*

CD 1, Tracks 71–75

GET THE MAIN IDEAS

Write T (true) or F (false).

CD 1, Tracks 71–75

1. **The Martinez family**
   ✓ They live on a ranch.
   ✓ Doña Maria has three children.
   ✓ Doña Maria is the head of the family.

2.  **The Abbot family**
   ✓ Glenn works in a bank.
   ✗ Liz works at the ~~Sydney~~ near Opera House.
   ✗ Alex and Louise are in college. school

3.  **The Feng family**
   ___ Shing travels a lot.
   ___ Mee Jin works at home.
   ___ Mingmei is 9, and Yuan is 6.

4. **The Eze family**
   ___ Aisha is the father.
   ___ Nneka teaches at a high school.
   ___ The Ezes have three daughters.

RESPOND TO THE IDEAS

Is your family like the Martinez family, the Abbot family, the Feng family, or the Eze family? Why?

WHAT IS YOUR FAMILY LIKE?

1. **Everyone's family is different. What is your family like? Look at the chart. Read the questions. Write your answers under "Me."**

Who in your family ... ?	Me 😊	Partner 1 😊	Partner 2 😊
watches a lot of TV?			
likes to cook?			
is kind of messy?			
is funny?			
likes to stay at home?			
likes to go out?			
is good at telling stories?			
wears nice clothes?			
loves to go shopping?			
is always busy?			
is easy to get money from?			
is the most fun to be around?			

2. **Talk to two classmates. Take turns asking questions. Fill in the chart.**

3. **Form groups. Tell your group two things you learned about each partner. Is anyone's family like yours?**

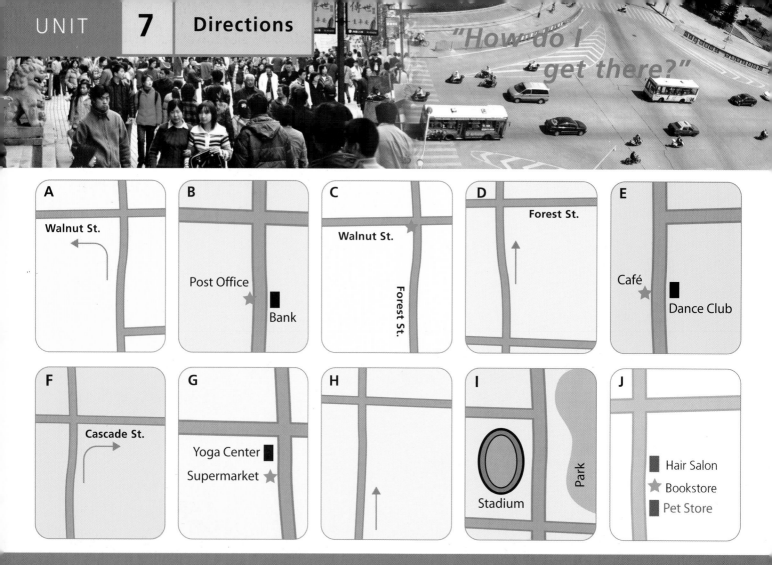

"How do I get there?"

A Walnut St.

B Post Office — Bank

C Walnut St. — Forest St.

D Forest St.

E Café — Dance Club

F Cascade St.

G Yoga Center — Supermarket

H

I Stadium — Park

J Hair Salon — Bookstore — Pet Store

Warm Up

Match the pictures to the sentences.

1. __H__ Go **straight**.
2. __D__ Go **down** the street to Forest Street.
3. __F__ **Take a right** on Cascade Street. → Turn right
4. __A__ **Turn left** on Walnut Street.
5. __C__ It's **on the corner** of Walnut and Forest.
6. __B__ The post office is **across from** the bank.
7. __J__ The bookstore is **between** the pet store and a hair salon.
8. __G__ The supermarket is **next to** the yoga center.
9. __E__ The café is **opposite** a dance club.
10. __I__ The stadium is **near** the park.

Now listen and check.

CD 1, Track 76

Think of a place (a shop, a park, a restaurant). Tell your partner how to get there from your school.

USEFUL EXPRESSIONS

How do you get to ... ?
I'm looking for ...
Excuse me. Where is ... ?
Sorry to bother you, but is there a ... close by?
How far is ... from here?

36

Look at the pictures. What are the people looking for?

 First Listening: What is each person trying to find?

CD 1, Tracks 77–81

☑ ATM (cash machine)
☐ a bank

☐ a restaurant
☐ a coffee shop

☐ a library
☐ a bookstore

☐ a yoga center
☐ a gym

 Second Listening: Where is each place?

CD 1, Tracks 77–81

1. ☑ about three blocks up
☐ in the next block up

2. ☐ near the park
☐ near the supermarket

3.  ☐ on Broad Street
☐ on Market Street

4.  ☐ on Sixth Street
☐ on Seventh Street

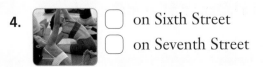

 Act out one of the conversations with a partner.

Real World Listening

PREPARE

 Lisa and a friend are visiting Brian in San Francisco. They ask him for his opinion about places to see. Find the places on the map.

Ghirardelli Square

Fisherman's Wharf

Coit Tower

Design: Reineck & Reineck San Francisco
© San Francisco Convention & Visitors Bureau 2002

 Now listen and follow the directions.

CD 1, Tracks 82–85

GET THE MAIN IDEAS

What does Brian say about each place?

CD 1, Track 82–85

Part 1	Ghirardelli Square	
Part 2	Fisherman's Wharf	Last Friday, Grammar teacher takes us go to chase bank.
Part 3	Coit Tower	

RESPOND TO THE IDEAS

38

What are the best places to visit in your city? Why?

WHERE IS IT?

1. Label the pictures with words from the box.

place to eat	vending machine	water fountain
laundromat	ATM	gas station
restroom	place to park	supermarket

2. Which location is the closest to your classroom? Which is the farthest? Rank the locations from 1–10. Write the numbers below the pictures.

Closest 1..10 Farthest

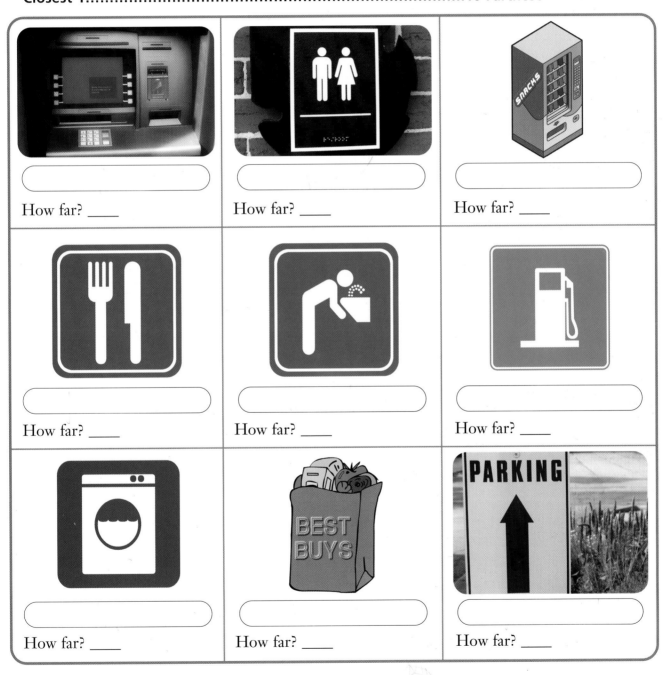

How far? _____   How far? _____   How far? _____

How far? _____   How far? _____   How far? _____

How far? _____   How far? _____   How far? _____

3. Pairwork. Give directions from your school to one of the places above. Have your partner guess the place. Take turns.

"*What kind of work do you do?*"

Warm Up

 Write two jobs in each column. (Use your own opinions.)

- [ ] video game programmer
- [ ] tour guide
- [ ] waiter
- [ ] engineer
- [✓] personal trainer
- [ ] sales representative
- [ ] flight attendant
- [ ] graphic designer
- [ ] bank teller
- [ ] doctor

helping people	talking to people	being creative
personal trainer		

🎧 **Now listen. Write the numbers you hear next to the jobs.**

CD 1, Track 86

USEFUL EXPRESSIONS

I've always wanted to ...
It's never boring.
I get to ...
I get tired of ...
I like being ...

 Which of these jobs would you like? Why? Tell your partner.

40

Look at the pictures. What do you think the jobs are?

First Listening: What does each person do?

CD 1, Tracks 87–91

1

☐ Doctor
☑ Nurse

2

☐ English teacher
☐ Math teacher

3

☐ Firefighter
☐ EMT (Emergency Medical Technician)

4

☐ Computer programmer
☐ Computer technician

Second Listening: Why do they like their jobs?

CD 1, Tracks 87–91

1. ☐ Likes to work at night
☑ Loves to help mothers

2. ☐ Likes to teach students
☐ Likes to work at night

3. ☐ Likes to hang out
☐ Likes to help people

4. ☐ Likes to be creative
☐ Likes to work alone

 Choose one of these jobs. Say why it would be OR wouldn't be a good job for you.

PREPARE

What is the right job for you? One way to find out is to take a quiz. Before you take the quiz, check the phrases below that you think describe you.

I like to

☐ be with people   ☐ be alone   ☐ be active

☐ be in charge   ☐ let people tell me what to do   ☐ be creative

☐ take risks   ☐ be careful

Now listen to the quiz and circle the answers that fit you best.

CD 1, Tracks 92–93

GET THE MAIN IDEAS

Make sure you circled the answers that fit you best.

CD 1, Tracks 92–93

WHICH JOB IS RIGHT FOR YOU?

	a	b	c
1.	bright pink	brown	green
2.	stay home and read	go snowboarding	visit an art museum
3.	IM your friends	go to a party	play computer games
4.	a fluffy, white cat	a snake	a goldfish
5.	practice yoga	go to a club with friends	go to bed
6.	put it in the bank	have a big party	take an art class
7.	read all of the instructions	just use it	read a few instructions
8.	keep quiet	say something	just forget about it
9.	get angry	call a friend to chat	relax and hang out
10.	finish, then call her back	talk to her as long as she needs to	tell her not to worry

RESPOND TO THE IDEAS

Find your score.
Give yourself:
3 points for each "a"
2 points for each "b"
1 point for each "c"

Totals:
over 25 points ••• You're very goal oriented. You might want to work at a bank.
20–25 points ••• You're ambitious and creative. You would be a good sales representative.
under 20 points ••• You like taking it easy. You could work as a computer technician.

Do you agree with your score? Compare with a partner.

Interaction Link

GET A JOB

1. Take turns asking each other the following questions about the jobs below. Mark your partner's answers in the chart. Give reasons for your answers.

   Is this job interesting or boring?

   Is this job easy or hard?

   Is this job important or unimportant?

Police officer	☐ interesting ☐ boring	☐ easy ☐ hard	☐ important ☐ unimportant
Graphic designer	☐ interesting ☐ boring	☐ easy ☐ hard	☐ important ☐ unimportant
Airline pilot	☐ interesting ☐ boring	☐ easy ☐ hard	☐ important ☐ unimportant
English teacher	☐ interesting ☐ boring	☐ easy ☐ hard	☐ important ☐ unimportant
Bus driver	☐ interesting ☐ boring	☐ easy ☐ hard	☐ important ☐ unimportant
Business manager	☐ interesting ☐ boring	☐ easy ☐ hard	☐ important ☐ unimportant
Musician	☐ interesting ☐ boring	☐ easy ☐ hard	☐ important ☐ unimportant
Software engineer	☐ interesting ☐ boring	☐ easy ☐ hard	☐ important ☐ unimportant
Tour guide	☐ interesting ☐ boring	☐ easy ☐ hard	☐ important ☐ unimportant
Yoga instructor	☐ interesting ☐ boring	☐ easy ☐ hard	☐ important ☐ unimportant

2. Groupwork. What kind of person do you have to be to do each job? Use words from the box below or other words you know.

warm	friendly	quiet	intelligent	creative	interesting
fun	confident	cool	artistic	helpful	calm

"I'm really busy these days."

Warm Up

 Mike has a busy life. Listen and write the days for each activity.

CD 2, Track 1

| Monday | Tuesday | Wednesday | Thursday | Friday | Saturday | Sunday |

1. Go to work: ___Tuesday, Thursday, Saturday___

2. Go to school: _____

3. Go to the gym: _____

4. Clean apartment: _____

5. Watch TV: _____

6. Hang out with friends: _____

7. Go out with girlfriend: _____

8. Chat on the computer: _____

Are you a busy person? Why or why not?

USEFUL EXPRESSIONS

What do you do on ... ?
What do you do in your free time?
How often do you ... ?
What are you up to on ... ?
I'm really busy.

44

👁 **Look at the pictures. What are these people doing?**

🎧 **First Listening:** **What activities are the speakers talking about?**

CD 2, Tracks 2–6

1

☑ starting a new job ☐ learning to swim

2

☐ watching a game ☐ playing video games

3

☐ buying books ☐ working at a bookstore

4

☐ getting in shape ☐ training for a race

🎧 **Second Listening:** **When do they do the activities?**

CD 2, Tracks 2–6

1. ☐ Tuesday
☑ Thursday

2. ☐ Sunday
☐ Monday

3. ☐ Sunday
☐ Monday

4. ☐ Thursday afternoon
☐ Thursday night

 Do you do any of these activities? Tell your partner.

ENJOY BEAUTIFUL AUSTRALIA!

to go home by car or in a car

"It was a fantastic trip!"

Warm Up

 Read the brochure. Write the missing words.

boat ~~go~~	foot	taxi
bus	horseback	train
flight	plane	
fly	swim	

AUSTRALIA

1. You'll start your week down under in Sydney, where you'll see the famous Sydney Opera House. You can ride the Sydney CityRail __**train**__ or take a __~~bus~~ taxi__ to all the popular sights.

2. From Sydney, you'll __*fly*__ north to Kununurra for a wildlife safari. You'll go down the Ord River by __*boat*__ and camp on the shores of Lake Argyle. Watch out for those crocodiles!

3. Next up is a two-day trip by air-conditioned __*taxi bus*__ to the middle of the Outback, where you'll see Uluru. If you'd like, you can rent a horse and explore the desert on __*horseback*__. Or, if you're up to it, you can explore by __*foot back*__.

4. After that, you'll go by __*plane*__ to the coast, where you'll see the Great Barrier Reef in a canoe. If you're adventurous, you can get in the water and __*swim*__ with the jellyfish.

5. After a short __*flight*__ back to Sydney, you'll be on your way back home.

 Now listen and check.
CD 2, Track 9

Tell a partner about an interesting trip you took.

48

👁 Look at the pictures. What are some popular travel spots to go to?

🎧 **First Listening:** What do the speakers remember about their trips? (Check more than one answer.)

CD 2, Tracks 10–12

1.
- ☐ the beaches
- ☑ the sunsets
- ☐ the weather
- ☐ the wildlife
- ☑ the people

2.
- ☐ the people
- ☑ the animals
- ☑ the weather
- ☐ the cities
- ☑ the stars   *humid*

🎧 **Second Listening:** Write T (true) or F (false).

CD 2, Tracks 10–12

Liz

Alicia

✓ She stayed for ten days.

✗ She went surfing.

✓ She rented a motorcycle.

✗ It's <u>dry</u> there.   *humid*

✓ She saw a jaguar.

✗ She was afraid.

There are ecotours to many places like the Pantanal or Costa Rica.
Would you like to do this kind of nature travel?

Real World Listening

PREPARE

 Jason Lewis is an adventurer from England. He is traveling around the world by "human power." Look at the pictures. Write the form of transportation in the boxes.

pedal boat   bicycle   inline skates   kayak

 Now listen to Part 1 and Part 2 and check.

CD 2, Tracks 13–14

GET THE MAIN IDEAS

 Listen to Part 1 again. Write the correct information.

CD 2, Track 14

England to Portugal

transportation

_____

Portugal to Florida

days to cross the Atlantic Ocean

_____

Florida to San Francisco

transportation

_____

San Francisco to Australia

days from San Francisco to Australia

_____

Australia

transportation

_____

Australia to Singapore

transportation

_____

RESPOND TO THE IDEAS

 Now listen to Part 2 again. What has Jason learned on his trip?

CD 2, Track 15

_____

Do you have a dream? What is it?

Interaction Link

TAKE A TRIP!

1. Work alone. Write the words and phrases in the chart.

bus	guest house	visit a museum	plane
hotel	go hiking	train	hostel
car	attend a festival	go shopping	homestay
campsite	try local foods	take photos	talk to locals

Transportation	Lodging	Highlight

2. Plan a trip around the world in pairs or groups. Include a lot of details in your plan!

Part 1	From:	To:
Transportation		
Lodging		
Highlight		
Part 2	From:	To:
Transportation		
Lodging		
Highlight		
Part 3	From:	To:
Transportation		
Lodging		
Highlight		
Part 4	From:	To:
Transportation		
Lodging		
Highlight		

"Where does it all go?"

Warm Up

👁 **What do different people say about money? Write the missing words.**

bargain	money	expensive	borrow
earn	cheap	save	debt
sale	afford	set aside	lend

1. I run out of ___money___ almost every month. I don't know how it happens.

2. I want to buy a new car, but I can't _____ it. I just don't make enough money.

3. I need $70 for a new pair of jeans. I wonder if my mom will _____ it to me.

4. These shoes are only $25. That is such a _____.

5. You paid $500 for a jacket? Are you crazy? That's way too _____!

6. I need to _____ some money. I'm spending too much.

7. My brother wants to _____ $10 from me. He never has any money.

8. This dress is so _____. It's only $30. I have to buy it!

9. I got an incredible deal on this cool phone. It was on _____. Check it out.

10. I'm always in _____. I need to stop using my credit cards all the time.

11. I _____ a lot at my job. The tips are great!

12. I want to _____ some money each month so I can take a trip next summer.

🎧 **Now listen and check.**

CD 2, Track 27

🗣 **How much money do you spend in a day? In a month? Is it too much?**

56

USEFUL EXPRESSIONS

How much does ... cost?

How much is ... ?

How much do you spend on ... ?

That's a great deal.

I can't afford it.

Look at the pictures. What money problems are they talking about?

 First Listening: **What do the people want to spend money on?**
CD 2, Tracks 28–32

1

☐ a trip   ☑ a car

2

☐ a new house   ☐ a trip

3

☐ clothes for a trip   ☐ clothes for a job

4

☐ a wedding   ☐ a honeymoon

 Second Listening: **How much do they need?**
CD 2, Tracks 28–32

1.   ☐ $20,000
                            ☑ $12,000

2.   ☐ $2,000
                            ☐ $3,000

3.   ☐ $400
                            ☐ $500

4.   ☐ $13,000
                            ☐ $30,000

 What do you do to save money?

"What do you want to do?"

MOVIE! MOVIE!

Warm Up

 Write the missing words.

| clubbing | let's go | feel like | want to | sound |
| quiet | to | going on | free | into |

1. I **feel like** going out tonight. Let's go somewhere fun.

2. I want to dance. How about going _____ tonight?

3. What are you up _____ this weekend? I'm in the mood to go hear some music.

4. I'm tired. I feel like going somewhere _____ tonight.

5. Are you _____ Saturday night? Let's have some fun after our exams are over.

6. I need to take a break from studying. _____ hang out somewhere.

7. I'm not really _____ shopping. I'm up for a movie or something, though.

8. Are you busy Sunday? How does the beach _____ to you?

9. Do you have anything _____ this Friday night? I'm having a party.

10. Do you _____ get together tomorrow? It's my day off.

Now listen and check.

CD 2, Track 35

USEFUL EXPRESSIONS

What do you think about a movie?
How about going to karaoke?
What about ordering a pizza?
Let's hang out at a coffee shop.
What are you up for tonight?

 Think of something to do with your partner.

Look at the pictures. What do you think they like to do for fun?

First Listening: What do they decide to do?

CD 2, Tracks 36–40

1

☑ go to dinner

☐ have some coffee

2

☐ study together

☐ take a break

3

☐ go to a party

☐ go dancing

4

☐ go to a comedy club

☐ go to a movie festival

Second Listening: What do they say?

CD 2, Tracks 36–40

1.  ☑ "I guess I can do that."
   ☐ "Sure, I'll do that."

2.  ☐ "I have to leave soon."
   ☐ "I can't stay long."

3.  ☐ "I guess I'm up for that."
   ☐ "I'd like to try that."

4. ☐ "OK, you win."
   ☐ "OK, I'll do it."

 How do you and your friends decide what to do?

61

Sofia
Bulgaria

Kaitlin
United States

Emi
Japan

PREPARE

Sofia, Kaitlin, and Emi are talking about what they like to do for fun. What do you think they will mention?

- [ ] go shopping
- [ ] be with friends
- [ ] go to movies
- [ ] chat online
- [ ] sing karaoke
- [ ] play video games
- [ ] go dancing
- [ ] go to clubs

Now listen and check.

CD 2, Tracks 41–44

GET THE MAIN IDEAS

Listen again. Check the things they like to do.

CD 2, Tracks 41–44

Sofia

- [ ] go to the movies
- [ ] play sports
- [ ] study
- [ ] watch TV
- [ ] hang out

Kaitlin

- [ ] go to the beach
- [ ] study
- [ ] go to the mall
- [ ] work at a café
- [ ] play sports

Emi

- [ ] go shopping
- [ ] go to the movies
- [ ] sing karaoke
- [ ] study
- [ ] go dancing

RESPOND TO THE IDEAS

Do you agree with Sofia that "it's the same everywhere"? What do you like to do with your friends?

WEEKEND FUN

1. You are the concierge for a major hotel in your city. The people below are in your city for the weekend. What do you recommend they do? Write two activities for each group.

recently married couple

1.
2.

business woman

1.
2.

high school students

1.
2.

airline flight crew

1.
2.

family of four

1.
2.

college graduates

1.
2.

2. Pairwork. Of the activities you planned, which one do you like the best? What group would be the most (or least) fun to hang out with? Tell your partner.

"She makes the best pasta."

Warm Up

 Look at the pictures and unscramble the words. list

1 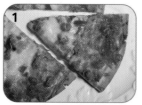	2 	3 	4 
zapiz	**stoopate**	**snabe & icre**	**knicech**
pizza	potatoes	beans&rice	chicken

5 	6 	7 	8 
gesg	**aspat**	**ladas**	**merna**
eggs	pasta	salad	ramen

9 	10 	11 	12 
doblett arwet	**geryne krind**	**burmeargh & nerfch risef**	**posu**
bottle water	energy drink	hamburger/french fries	soup

13 	14 	15 	16 
spich	**clespik**	**usish**	**eschee**
chips	pickles	sushi	cheese

 Now listen and check.

CD 2,
Track 45

 What do you usually eat for lunch?
What's your favorite snack?
Tell your partner.

USEFUL EXPRESSIONS

I'd like a bottle of water.
My favorite food is pizza.
That tastes good.
This is delicious.
She makes the best pasta.

Look at the pictures. What are the people eating?

hambuag

1

2

3

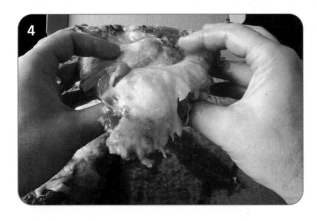

4

First Listening: Write + for the things the speakers like and – for the things they don't like.

CD 2, Tracks 46–50

1. [+] rice and vegetables
   [–] a hamburger
   [ ] shrimp

2. [–] chicken soup
   [+] vegetable soup
   [ ] noodle soup

3. [–] potatoes
   [+] salad
   [+] cucumbers

4. [–] pizza
   [+] pasta
   [ ] bread

Second Listening: Why doesn't the speaker like one of the foods?

CD 2, Tracks 46–50

1. [ ] it's too salty
   [✓] it's too heavy
   [ ] it's too greasy

2. [ ] the color
   [ ] the smell
   [✓] the taste

3. [ ] how it tastes
   [ ] how it looks
   [✓] how it feels

4. [ ] too much tomato
   [✓] too much cheese
   [ ] too much meat

What are your favorite fast foods?

PREPARE

 Enrico has a cooking show. Today he is teaching us to make pizza. What will he tell us to do? Order the steps 1–5.

___ Add the toppings   _1_ Prepare the dough

___ Spread the sauce   _5_ Enjoy it with friends

___ Bake the pizza

 Now listen and check.

CD 2, Tracks 51–55

GET THE MAIN IDEAS

 Number the steps in each part.

CD 2, Tracks 51–55

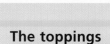

The dough	The sauce	The toppings
_2_ Cover the dough	_3_ Spread the sauce	_3_ Put oil on the toppings
_1_ Mix the dough	_2_ Choose a sauce	_1_ Choose your toppings
_3_ Wait an hour	_1_ Spread some oil	_2_ Sprinkle toppings on the pizza
_4_ Stretch into a big circle		_4_ Bake the pizza

 What kind of pizza would you like to try?

66

FOOD HABITS

1. Work alone. Read the questions in the survey. Check "Yes" or "No." If you answer "Yes," complete the sentence.

1. Do you eat breakfast?
   - ☐ No, I don't.
   - ☑ Yes, I usually have ___eggges and bread.___

2. Do you eat lunch?
   - ☐ No, I don't.
   - ☑ Yes, I usually have ___rice and chicken.___

3. Do you like fruit?
   - ☐ No, I don't.
   - ☑ Yes, I do. My favorite fruit is ___aple___ .

4. Do you eat snacks?
   - ☐ No, I don't.
   - ☑ Yes, I do. I like _____ .

5. Do you have a favorite food?
   - ☐ No, I don't.
   - ☑ Yes, I do. It's _____ .

6. Is there any food you don't like and won't eat?
   - ☐ No, there isn't.
   - ☑ Yes, there is. It's _____ .

7. Do you have a favorite restaurant?
   - ☐ No, I don't.
   - ☐ Yes, I do. It's _____ . (name of restaurant)

8. Do you know how to cook anything?
   - ☐ No, I don't.
   - ☐ Yes, I can make _____ .

   You need to use _____, _____, _____ .

   The steps are _____, _____, _____ .

2. Ask your partner the questions. Have him or her give reasons for the answers. If your partner answers "Yes" to 8, ask him or her to tell you how to make it.

"How are you feeling?"

Warm Up

 What health problem does each person have? Write the missing words and phrases.

earache	sore throat	backache	headache	stomachache	cough	stressed

耳痛

1. *What's the matter? You look awful.*
   I have a bad ___stomachache___. My stomach's been upset all morning.

2. *What's wrong?*
   I have an _____. My ear is killing me.

3. *How's your cold?*
   A lot better. I still have a _____ and a _____, though.

4. *Did that medicine help your _____?*
   No, not really. I feel like my head's going to split.

5. *Are you OK?*
   I have a terrible _____. It hurts to move.

6. *What's up? You look tired.*
   I'm really tense. I'm so _____ about my classes.

 Now listen and check.

CD 2, Track 56

Ask your partner about his or her health.

> **USEFUL EXPRESSIONS**
> What's the matter?
> What's wrong?
> How are you feeling?
> What's the problem?
> Are you all right?

Listening Task

👁 **Look at the pictures. What's wrong with the people?**

1

🎧 CD 2, Tracks 57–60

First Listening:
What is the problem?

1. ☐ a headache
   ☐ a cold
   ☑ a sore throat

2. ☐ a fever
   ☐ a backache
   ☐ a stomachache

3. ☐ stress
   ☐ a sore throat
   ☐ sore muscles

2

🎧 CD 2, Tracks 57–60

Second Listening:
What does the friend say to do?

1. ☐ have some soup
   ☑ drink some tea

2. ☐ take some pain pills
   ☐ take a hot bath

3. ☐ get a massage
   ☐ take a walk in the park

3

👄 **Your friend has a bad cold. What do you tell your friend to do?**

69

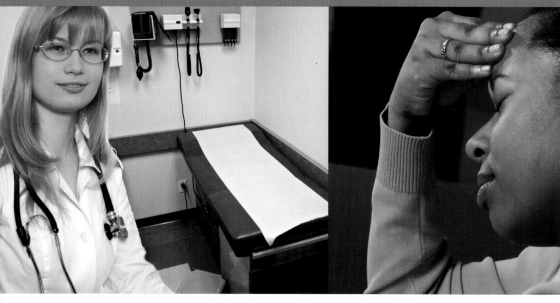

PREPARE

Dr. Helen Monroe works at a student health clinic. Students visit her about their health problems. Check the problems you think students talk to her about.

- [ ] fever
- [ ] stomachache
- [ ] homework

- [ ] stress
- [ ] allergy
- [ ] flu

- [ ] roommates
- [ ] headache
- [ ] sore throat

Now listen and check.

CD 2, Tracks 61–63

GET THE MAIN IDEAS

What is the problem? What does she say to do? Check your answers.

CD 2, Tracks 61–63

	Part 1 Tina	**Part 2** Ramon
What is the problem?	[ ] a fever [ ] a headache	[ ] an allergy [ ] a cold
What does she say to do?	[ ] go to bed earlier [ ] drink less coffee [ ] drink more water [ ] eat less at lunch	[ ] drink tea and juice [ ] eat more [ ] rest [ ] drink lots of water

RESPOND TO THE IDEAS

Have you had any of these health problems? What did you do?

70

WHAT DO YOU TAKE FOR THAT?

1. Ask a partner these questions.

Problem	Do you usually take modern medicine for this?	What is a good traditional remedy for this?
Headache	☐ Yes ☐ No	
Toothache	☐ Yes ☐ No	
Burn	☐ Yes ☐ No	
Rash	☐ Yes ☐ No	
Cut	☐ Yes ☐ No	
Cold	☐ Yes ☐ No	
Fever	☐ Yes ☐ No	
Sore throat	☐ Yes ☐ No	
Stomachache	☐ Yes ☐ No	
Hangover	☐ Yes ☐ No	

2. Groupwork. Compare your charts. Share ideas on what to do for these problems.

"I love it here."

Warm Up

Read what different people say about their hometowns. What do they like (+)? What do they dislike (–)?

1. ☐+☐ There are some good **restaurants**.

2. ☐ There isn't good **public transportation**.

3. ☐ There's a lot of **things to do**.

4. ☐ The **schools** aren't very good.

5. ☐ There's a lot of **nature**. We have some beautiful **parks**.

6. ☐ It's very **safe**. There isn't much **crime**.

7. ☐ It's too **crowded**. The **traffic's** pretty bad.

8. ☐ It's not very clean. There's too much **pollution**.

9. ☐ The **shopping** is great. There are so many stores to choose from.

10. ☐ There's a great mix of **old and modern buildings**.

11. ☐ There's always something **happening**.

12. ☐ The **people** are really friendly.

Now listen and check.

CD 2, Track 64

> USEFUL EXPRESSIONS
>
> What do you like about ... ?
> What do you like about living in ... ?
> Is there anything you don't like?
> There's a lot to do there.
> There's always something happening.

72 **Tell your partner one thing you like and one thing you don't like about your hometown.**

Look at the pictures. What looks interesting in these cities?

 First Listening: What does each speaker like about the city?

CD 2, Tracks 65–69

1 Vancouver, Canada

☑ the people
☐ the weather

2 Mexico City, Mexico

☐ the shopping
☐ the art and culture

3 Rio, Brazil

☐ the music
☐ the weather

4 London, England

☐ the food
☐ the people

 Second Listening: Which season does the speaker talk about?

CD 2, Tracks 65–69 (spring, summer, fall, winter)

1.  Winter

2.

3.

4.

 What's your favorite season where you live?
What do you like about it?

73

Real World Listening

New York, USA

Brisbane, Australia

Edinburgh, Scotland

PREPARE

Three students are talking about studying abroad. What do you think they will mention?

- [ ] the weather
- [ ] the shopping
- [ ] the cultural events
- [ ] the people
- [ ] the parks
- [ ] the buildings

Now listen and check.

CD 2, Tracks 70–73

GET THE MAIN IDEAS

Write T (true) or F (false) next to each statement.

CD 2, Tracks 70–73

Seri

Pieter

Carla

___ "I felt very safe."

___ "The weather wasn't bad."

___ "I made friends from all over the world."

___ "The public transportation was pretty bad."

___ "I didn't like Central Park."

___ "It's really relaxed there."

___ "There are a lot of nice places to hang out."

___ "There aren't many parks."

___ "It was way too hot."

___ "It was really dangerous."

___ "The weather isn't great."

___ "The festivals were boring."

___ "There are so many wonderful old buildings."

___ "People helped me when I got lost."

___ "It's easy to get around."

RESPOND TO THE IDEAS

Which of the three cities would you like to go to?

74

THE BEST CITY FOR ...

1. Work alone. Answer these questions.

What is the ...	in your country?	in the world?
biggest city		
most beautiful city		
oldest city		
most expensive city		
cheapest city		
best city to work in		
best city to raise a family in		
best city for nightlife		
best city for public transportation		
best city to meet foreign people		
best place to eat great food		
best place to see a sporting event		
best place for affordable housing		
best city to retire in		

2. Share your answers with a partner. See if you agree or disagree.

3. Groupwork. Compare your charts. Decide on the best place to live. Give reasons.

PART 2. Understanding conversations.

🎧 **Listen to each conversation. Then circle the answers.**

CD 2, Tracks 75–84

1. What does he want to save money for?

   (a) A trip to Europe.

   (b) A trip to Spain.

   (c) Plane tickets to Europe.

2. Why does she need to buy new clothes?

   (a) She doesn't like her old clothes.

   (b) She likes shopping.

   (c) She got a new job.

3. What does she want to do?

   (a) She doesn't want to do anything.

   (b) She wants to stay home.

   (c) She wants to stay out late.

4. Where are they going to meet?

   (a) At a coffee shop.

   (b) At a restaurant.

   (c) At the library.

5. Why doesn't she like hamburgers?

   (a) Hamburgers are too light.

   (b) Hamburgers are too simple.

   (c) Hamburgers are too heavy.

6. What does his grandmother do?

    (a) His grandmother makes delicious pasta.

    (b) His grandmother makes delicious pizza.

    (c) His grandmother eats a lot.

7. What did Sandy do?

    (a) Sandy hurt her foot.

    (b) Sandy hurt her leg.

    (c) Sandy hurt her back.

8. What's wrong with Ramon?

    (a) Ramon has a sore throat.

    (b) Ramon has a stomachache.

    (c) Ramon has a cough.

9. What does he think of Canadians?

    (a) Canadians are unfriendly.

    (b) Canadians are friendly.

    (c) Canadians are very cold.

10. What is the summer like in Rio?

    (a) The summer in Rio is cold.

    (b) The summer in Rio is hot.

    (c) The summer in Rio is warm.

Listen to the conversations. Write the missing words.

Self-Study CD, Track 2

Part 1

Tomas: Hey, Eddie! How's it going?

Eddie: Not bad. How are you _doing_?

Tomas: Pretty good.

Eddie: So how was your summer?

Tomas: Mm, it was all right.

Eddie: Cool.

Tomas: Hey, where are you living this year?

Eddie: Oh, I got an _apartment_ with some friends.

Tomas: Nice.

Eddie: What _about_ you? Where are you living?

Tomas: Eh, I'm in the dorms again.

Eddie: Dorms. That's not too bad.

Tomas: No, it works.

Part 2

Tomas: Hey, how's it going?

Yuki: Oh, _hey_. You're in this class too?

Tomas: Yeah.

Yuki: Do you think it's going to be hard?

Tomas: Hmm. I don't know. I _hope_ not.

Yuki: Yeah, me too.

Tomas: So …

Yuki: Oh, here he _comes_.

Tomas: Who?

Yuki: The teacher.

Tomas: Oh, well, talk to you later, OK?

Part 3

Tomas: Um, Dr. Collins?

Dr. Collins: Yes? Can I help you with _something_?

Tomas: Um, yes. Um, is there, um. Do you have room in your psychology class?

Dr. Collins: Hmm. Psychology. Which class?

Tomas: The one on Monday and Wednesday. 10 to 11.

Dr. Collins: Psychology 103. Hmm. Yes, I think I have _room_ in that one. You're in luck.

Tomas: Oh, great. I want to add the class. Can you _sign_ this?

Dr. Collins: Sure. There you go.

Tomas: Thanks, Dr. Collins.

Dr. Collins: You're welcome. I'll _see_ you on Wednesday.

BONUS QUESTION

Do you think Tomas and Yuki will talk after class? Write their conversation.

I think Tomas and Yuki will talk about their class and their teacher. They think their class is very good and classmate is very friendly, their teacher is very serious-

Unit 2 Self-Study

🎧 **Listen to the conversations. Write the missing words.**

Self-Study CD, Track 4

Part 1

Ronda: OK, Tim, I found two _rental_ apartments that look pretty good. Can you take a look?
Tim: OK, show me.
Ronda: Here, look. This one is on York Drive, $950 a month, _furnished_.
Tim: Hmm. $950? I like this one.
Ronda: So here's the inside, and a big kitchen, new _appliances_, big fridge, new gas stove.
Tim: Hmm, I like that.
Ronda: OK, it also says there's one bedroom, and that it comes with a king-size bed. And there's a new sofa in the living room.
Tim: New sofa, that's good. Nice. What else?
Ronda: Wood _floors_. No carpets.
Tim: Mm, that's good, I think.
Ronda: Yeah. Oh, here's the map. The _location_ is kind of weird. Look, it's on a really busy street.
Tim: I don't know.
Ronda: Yeah, it'd be noisy.

Part 2

Ronda: So, here's the other apartment. This one's on Garden Street, $850 a month.
Tim: That's _reasonable_. Garden Street. That's a good location, near the lake. What's it like?
Ronda: One bedroom. It looks small.
Tim: Furnished?
Ronda: Yes. Looks like there's a big couch and a table in the _living_ room.
Tim: What else?
Ronda: Um, the bed's kind of small.
Tim: Yeah, looks like it.
Ronda: Ah. Here's a shot of the _bathroom_.
Tim: Ooh, kind of small for both of us, don't you think?
Ronda: Hmm, and that bathtub is kind of old. You know I like to take baths.
Tim: Yeah, I know you do.
Ronda: And—ouch! The kitchen looks tiny.
Tim: And kind of old appliances. Not so good for cooking.
Ronda: Yeah, but it's got a little _antique_ table and two chairs.
Tim: That's all we need, really.
Ronda: Yeah, it's kind of cute. What else?
Tim: Oh, here's the living room, new carpet, and it's got a lot of windows, and this says there's a nice _balcony_.
Ronda: Hmm …

BONUS QUESTION

What do Tim and Ronda decide to do? Write the rest of their conversation.

Listen to the conversation. Write the missing words.

Jake: Tell me, what do people wear at clubs in your country?

Jenny: You mean dance clubs?

Jake: Yeah, what do young people wear?

Jenny: These days, kids want to be _sexy_ .

Jake: Sexy? What do you mean?

Jenny: I mean, like wearing a tank top, a top that shows a lot of your skin.

Jake: OK, showing a lot of skin. That's sexy, huh?

Jenny: Yeah.

Jake: What about guys? What do guys usually wear?

Jenny: Guys? They wear casual cargo pants and maybe a polo shirt.

Jake: A polo shirt?

Jenny: Or maybe a cool T-shirt. Some kind of cool _logo_ on it.

Jake: OK, do girls wear cargo pants, too?

Jenny: No, no, never. Girls like short _skirts_ , or jeans, and of course high heels.

Jake: High heels! Aren't high heels hard to dance in?

Jenny: They are actually, but we look so much better with high heels on. We look taller. That's good.

Jake: How about guys? What kind of shoes do they wear?

Jenny: Usually _sneakers_ .

Jake: Well, how about jewelry? Do you wear any kind of jewelry, or _accessories_ necklaces?

Jenny: I personally don't wear a necklace, but lots of people do. I always wear _earrings_ . Big hoops. Silver ones. Those look really pretty at the clubs. Very _shiny_ .

Jake: How about makeup?

Jenny: Oh, of course. Makeup is really important, too.

Jake: Ah, I see.

Jenny: Like makeup for eyelashes. You want to have a really strong _look_ for your eyes.

Jake: _lipstick_ ?

Jenny: Definitely. Shiny lip-gloss looks good in the lights, you know.

Jake: Do guys wear makeup too?

Jenny: I don't think so. Not at the clubs I go to. But they wear _perfume_. Or how do you say it?

Jake: Uh, cologne.

Jenny: Yeah, cologne. I actually like it when guys wear cologne.

Jake: Well, it sounds like you have a lot of fun at the clubs.

Jenny: Oh, yeah. It's a lot of fun. Dressing up, meeting people, talking, laughing, dancing.

BONUS QUESTION

What do you think Jenny wears to school? Write the conversation.

Unit 4 Self-Study

🎧 **Listen to the conversations. Write the missing words.**

Self-Study CD, Track 8

Part 1

Rachel: Hi. Is this seat taken?

Hiro: No, it's free.

Rachel: Thanks.

Hiro: Oh, you're from the _States_ ?

Rachel: Yes, I'm from San Francisco.

Hiro: Ah, I love San Francisco.

Rachel: Are you _American_?

Hiro: No, I'm Japanese, but I lived in the States before.

Rachel: You're Japanese then?

Hiro: Right.

Rachel: What part of Japan are you from?

Hiro: I'm from Kyushu in _western_ Japan.

Rachel: I learned this one expression in Japanese. Yoroshiku. How's my pronunciation?

Hiro: Um, not bad.

Part 2

Rachel: Excuse me. Do you know which stop is for the Tower of London?

Miguel: Sorry. Sorry. I don't. I'm just a _visitor_ here.

Rachel: Oh, I'm visiting, too.

Miguel: I can get my _guidebook_. Hang on. Tower of London. That's the next stop, Tower Hill.

Rachel: Thanks.

Miguel: So you're from the States.

Rachel: Yes, San Francisco. How about you?

Miguel: I'm _Mexican_. I'm from Monterrey.

Rachel: Oh, cool. Well, how do you like London?

Miguel: It's great. Oh, here's your stop.

Rachel: Thanks. See you.

Part 3

Rachel: Excuse me. Excuse me. You dropped your map.

Silvia: Oh, oh. Thank you.

Rachel: Are you a _tourist_, too?

Silvia: Yes, I am. I'm from _Italy_.

Rachel: Oh, interesting. Are you from _Rome_?

Silvia: No, I'm from _Florence_.

Rachel: Oh, I see. And are you going to visit the Tower of London?

Silvia: Yes, I am. Come on. Let's walk together.

Rachel: What do you think of London so far?

Silvia: I think it is fabulous.

BONUS QUESTION

What do you think Rachel and Silvia talk about while they walk around London? Write the conversation.

Listen to the show. Write the missing words.

Self-Study CD, Track 10

Hello, everyone, and welcome to People Bingo. I'm your host, Cliff Parker. Here's how the game works. I give the clues, you guess the _person_. Make an X on the square, and if you get three in a _row_, that's Bingo! And you win the game. Are you ready? Well, ready or not, it's time to start People Bingo! Let's begin.

First, this person is tall and _thin_ and is wearing _jeans_ and a T-shirt. The T-shirt is white with blue _sleeves_. And she has very long hair.

Next, this person has short, dark hair and is wearing a pair of white shorts, and he has on a blue _Hawaiian_ shirt with flowers on it.

Next, this person has _long_ dark hair, and she's wearing a black _dress_ and a white sweater over it.

Next, this person has blond hair and is wearing jeans, and he's also wearing a white sweater.

Next, this person is wearing _baggy_ jeans and a red T-shirt. He's also wearing a _red_ cap.

And we have a winner. Congratulations!

BONUS QUESTION
Write the script for round number two.

Listen to the show. Write the missing words.

Self-Study CD, Track 12

Hi, everyone. This is Eva Stone of *World Encounters*. Today's world encounter is world families."
Let's go around the world and look at some different families.

Meet the Martinez family. They're from Honduras, in Central America. They live on a cattle ranch
in the countryside. There are five people living at the ranch. Doña Maria is the mother and the
head of the _household_ She has a son named Miguel. He lives on the ranch with his _wife_,
Maria. Miguel and Maria have a son named Carlos, who's 12, and a daughter, Gabriella, who is 8.
Doña Maria also has two other _children_.

Meet the Abbot family. They're from Sydney, Australia. There are five _people_ in their family:
the father, Glenn, the mother, Liz, their older daughter, Beth, the son, Alex, and the _younger_
daughter, Louise. Glenn works at a bank in downtown Sydney. Liz runs a little café near the
Sydney Opera House. Alex and Louise are in high school. They love to surf, and there are so many
great beaches near Sydney! Here are the Abbots, with Glenn's _parents_, Daniel and Ruth, and
his aunt Greta.

Meet the Feng family. They live in Shanghai, China, in a high-rise building, in Puxi, along the
Yangzi River. Shing, the _father_, works for a trading company. He's very busy. He travels a lot
to Singapore, Hong Kong, and other Asian cities. Mee Jin, the _mother_, works at home. She has
a _home_ office and does design work for a textile company. The Fengs have two children,
Yuan, who's 9, and Mingmei, who's 6.

Meet the Eze family. They're from Nigeria. There are many people in their _extended_ family, but
this is the _immediate_ family that lives together in Lagos. The father is Chuka. He is a doctor at a
hospital. The mother is Nneka. She is a teacher at the high school nearby. They have two
daughters. Chizoba. She is 14 years old. And Aisha. She's 12. They are both students.

Well, thanks for joining us today. If you have an idea for *World Encounters*, please e-mail us.

BONUS QUESTION
What would Eva Stone say about your family? Write the script.

Listen to the conversations. Write the missing words and phrases.

Self-Study CD, Track 14

Part 1

Lisa: So, Brian, we want to see some of San Francisco this afternoon. Do you have any suggestions?

Brian: Oh, you want to be tourists, huh?

Lisa: Yeah, sure.

Brian: Well, you can _____ at Ghirardelli Square.

Lisa: Is it far?

Brian: No, no, it's really _____. Here's a map. Just walk down Larkin Street to North Point Street. It's right there, just about six or seven _____.

Lisa: OK, that sounds easy.

Part 2

Lisa: And how about Fisherman's Wharf?

Brian: You want to see Fisherman's Wharf? Yeah, sure. Why not? You can have some great _____ from there.

Lisa: Can we walk?

Brian: Sure. You can walk to that, too. Just walk _____ Jefferson Street. Fisherman's Wharf is right at the end of Jefferson Street. Can't miss it. It's full of tourists!

Part 3

Lisa: OK, how about Coit Tower? I hear that's a famous _____ in San Francisco.

Brian: Yeah, yeah. It is. It's kind of neat.

Lisa: How do we get there?

Brian: Uh, let's see this map. It's on the _____ of Telegraph Hill, here.

Lisa: Yeah, I see it.

Brian: So you have to walk along the Embarcadero, OK? To Lombard Street, and then _____ right and walk up the _____. It's easy to see from _____.

Lisa: Great. Do you have any other ideas for us?

Brian: Well, you know what's nice? You ought to visit North Beach. Just walk along Columbus Avenue.

BONUS QUESTION

Brian, Lisa, and her friend have dinner together. What do they talk about? Write the conversation.

Listen to the quiz. Write the missing words.

Self-Study CD, Track 16

1. Choose one of these colors:

   (a) _____   (b) _____   (c) _____

2. It's a snowy, winter day. Do you … ?

   (a) _____   (b) _____   (c) _____

3. It's Saturday night. You are free. Do you … ?

   (a) _____   (b) _____   (c) _____

4. You want a pet. Do you buy … ?

   (a) _____   (b) _____   (c) _____

5. It's 11 o'clock at night. Do you … ?

   (a) _____   (b) _____   (c) _____

6. You have some extra money. Do you … ?

   (a) _____   (b) _____   (c) _____

7. You buy a new camera. Do you … ?

   (a) _____   (b) _____   (c) _____

8. Your friend does something that makes you angry. Do you … ?

   (a) _____   (b) _____   (c) _____

9. You have to wait in a long line at the airport. Do you … ?

   (a) _____   (b) _____   (c) _____

10. You need to finish your homework. A friend calls. She has a serious problem. Do you … ?

   (a) _____   (b) _____   (c) _____

BONUS QUESTION

Would you answer any of the questions above differently? Write the answers.

Listen to the conversations. Write the missing words.

Self-Study CD, Track 18

Monday morning

Celia: OK, Ms. Abbot, I'll get that report for you right _____. And by the way, Don Wilson
called earlier. He said he'll be a little _____ for your 11 o'clock meeting.

Tuesday afternoon

Tracy: So then, I don't know what to do now, Celia.
Celia: Just forget about him. You can find another boyfriend. He's a _____ for doing that to you.
Tracy: I know, but I still kind of like him.

Wednesday afternoon

Answering machine: You have reached the office of Dr. Patel. The office is closed right _____.
If you would like to _____ an appointment, please press 1 now. If this is a
medical emergency, please press 2.

Thursday evening

Clerk: Is that it?
Celia: Yes.
Clerk: Do you want _____ or plastic?
Celia: Please put the milk, the eggs, and the bread in paper. The bananas and the rest can go in plastic.

Friday night

Craig: I had a great time tonight.
Celia: I did, too, Craig. The movie was really funny.
Craig: So, are you going to _____ me in?
Celia: No, sorry. You know the rules. I'll call you tomorrow, OK?
Craig: OK.
Celia: G'night.
Craig: G'night.

Saturday morning

Stylist: So, how do you want your hair cut?
Celia: I'm not sure. I need a new look.
Sylist: How about if I take a little off here, and cut it shorter in the _____?
Celia: OK.

Sunday morning

Celia: That was a killer _____.
Shawna: No kidding.
Celia: I think I'll _____ the gym tomorrow.
Shawna: Come on.

BONUS QUESTION

What other people do you think Celia talks to? Write another conversation.

Listen to the show. Write the missing words.

Self-Study CD, Track 20

Part 1

Steven: Welcome to Global Trek. I'm Steven Morris, and today I'm in Singapore with special guest Jason Lewis. Jason is on a round-the-world trip using just human power. He started in England and went by bicycle through Europe down to Portugal, and then across the Atlantic Ocean in a special pedal boat. Using no motors, no sails, just human power. This part of the trip took 111 days. Then Jason traveled by inline skates across the U.S., from Florida to California. The next leg of the trip, from San Francisco to Australia, was the longest part of the trip so far. San Francisco to Hawaii was 53 days, and then from Hawaii to Australia was 126 days. All in his special pedal boat, the *Moksha*. Then Jason traveled through Australia by bicycle and then up the Indonesian coast to Singapore by kayak. Wow, what an incredible trip!

Part 2

Steven: What __made__ you decide to do this?

Jason: Other people have gone __around__ the world, but no one has done it this way. I wanted to be the first to do it by human power alone.

Steven: Well, now we're in Singapore. What is the __route__ from here?

Jason: Well, we're going to go by bicycle up through Thailand, China, and India. And then __work__ my way back to Europe. Back to my __starting__ point in England.

Steven: How?

Jason: By bicycle all the __way__ to France, and then pedal boat again across the English Channel.

Steven: Wow! And how long do you __figure__ it will take you?

Jason: I have no idea. When I started, I thought maybe five or six years __total__. But it's been longer than that, and I'm not __done__ yet!

Steven: Any regrets?

Jason: Nope, none at all. It's been incredible. I've learned so much about the world and about myself. I've met so many great people.

Steven: Well, it's been a pleasure talking to you, Jason. Good luck on the __rest__ of your trip.

Jason: Thanks.

BONUS QUESTION

What will Jason say when he returns to England? Write the interview.

Listen to the conversations. Write the missing words.

Self-Study CD, Track 22

Sarah: Good morning. I'd like a large coffee and a bagel.
Clerk: That'll be $_____.

Sarah: Let's see. The fare to downtown is $_____. Can I have one ticket to downtown?
Clerk: That's $_____.

Sarah: Hmm. The lunch special today is pizza with a small salad and a drink for $_____.
 I think I'll get that.
Alice: That's a good deal. $_____. I'll get that, too.

Sarah: I'd like a ticket for the 8 o'clock show.
Ticket clerk: That's _____.

Sarah: Let's take a taxi home. It's so late, and I'm so tired. Taxi!
Sarah: Please take us to 56th and Broadway.
Driver: Sure.

Driver: Here you go.
Sarah: How much is the fare?
Driver: It's $_____.
Sarah: Here's a _____. Thanks. Good night.

BONUS QUESTION
What do you spend money on each week? Write about it.

Listen to the speakers. Write the missing words.

Self-Study CD, Track 24

Part 1

Sofia: So, at home in Bulgaria I like to go out and be with my friends, you know, have fun. We are all so ___busy___ with school and all, studying all the time, so then on the weekend we like to get together and do something. We go to movies or we go shopping, you know, just walk ___around___ and look at the stores to see the latest fashions, what clothes to wear. Or sometimes we play sports, like swimming or tennis. And sometimes we do ___nothing___, you know, we just hang out and talk and _____ and not think about anything important. My parents are really strict. They want me to study hard all the time. So when I have a little free time, I like to hang out with my friends and do something fun. Laugh. I think it's the same everywhere, isn't it?

Part 2

Kaitlin: Yeah, I guess it's the same. I live near Los Angeles. My friends and I, we studied pretty hard, but not so much, really. I mean, we got OK grades, but we weren't studying all the time. My parents weren't happy about that. They got angry with me, but I don't know. I'm more of an ___action___ person. I like to get out, do stuff, have some fun, be with people. I just can't study all the time, so I had a ___part time___ job at a café for a couple of years. Yeah, so, anyway, my friends and I, we all like to hang out _____. We go to movies or _____ at the mall and, uh, we go to the beach a lot.

Part 3

Emi: For me, it's kind of similar. My friends and I, we all study a lot. And on the ___weekend___, it's about the same. I hang out with friends, go to movies, or go shopping. Oh, and go to karaoke. We all like to go to karaoke and sing really loud, especially after a big exam. We _____ the exam and we just go and _____ really loud and laugh and forget about school. It feels great! Sometimes we go to dance _____ on the weekends. I don't go very often, but some of my friends do. We are so busy with school, so I like to be with friends when I can.

BONUS QUESTION
What do you think a young person on another planet would do for fun? Write about it.

Listen to the show. Write the missing words.

Part 1

Do you like pizza? Today, I want to show you how to make delicious pizza. Many people hear the word *pizza* and they think tomato _sauce_ and cheese, right? But today I want to show you how pizza has gone international. You can also make Thai, Chinese, _Greek_, any kind of pizza you want. I'll show you how. It's fun. It's easy. First off, for any pizza there are three basic _steps_: the dough, then the sauce, and then the toppings, OK? Are you ready? Let's get started.

Part 2

So let's start with the dough. You can use this dough for any pizza. To make the dough we need 1 cup of water, 3 cups of _flour_, a tablespoon each of sugar and salt, and yeast. Oh, and a little oil. First we mix the dough. We mix everything together. Mix it well. Then, put the dough in a _bowl_ and cover it. Wait about one hour. Look at the dough. Does it look bigger, kind of like a little pillow? Then it's ready.

Next comes the fun part. You take the dough and make it into a big circle. Use your hands. Push it, and _pull_ it, and stretch it until it's a big circle. This looks easy to do. It's a little tricky. Don't worry. You'll do fine. Practice makes perfect.

Part 3

Then comes the sauce. I'll start with a traditional Italian pizza with tomato sauce. You take some tomato sauce and spread the tomato sauce all over. Remember, I said before, you can make any kind of pizza: Italian, Chinese, Thai. OK, so this is where it gets fun. Say you want to make a pizza with Chinese _ingredients_ You can use hoisin sauce instead. How about a Thai pizza? You can use _peanut_ sauce. You can choose the taste you like.

Now, listen up. This next step is very important for good pizza. For any sauce, spread a little oil first, then the sauce. Remember: oil, then sauce. Oh, and don't use too much sauce. That makes the dough _wet_.

Part 4

Next comes the toppings. For toppings, again, you can use whatever you want: strips of chicken, slices of _mushroom_ or sausage, onions, shrimp, pineapple, _vegetable_, cheese, whatever you like. One time I even had a Korean-like pizza with a little bit of bulgogi—grilled beef—on it. They served it with kimchi! It was fantastic! Anyway, just sprinkle the toppings all over.

OK, now put a little bit of oil on the toppings, the shrimp or vegetables, whatever toppings you used. Just a little bit so it's not too dry.

Finally, we are all set to bake the pizza. Bake the pizza for about 20 minutes in a very hot _oven_. And that's it. Your pizza is ready to eat. Sounds easy? It is. Give some to your friends. They'll love it! That's all for today. Until next time, *ciao a tutti!*

BONUS QUESTION

Do you know how to cook something? Write a recipe.

🎧 **Listen to the conversation. Write the missing words.**

Self-Study CD, Track 28

Part 1

Receptionist: Tina Rogers? Tina? Hi, how are you? Come this way.

Dr. Monroe: Hi. Let's see, Tina. What's the _matter_?

Tina: Well, I have a lot of headaches. I get a bad headache almost every day, in the afternoon.

Dr. Monroe: You get a headache every day?

Tina: Yeah, just about.

Dr. Monroe: OK. First off, many people get headaches. It's probably nothing _serious_, but we need to find out why you _get_ them. Do you drink a lot of water?

Tina: Um, I drink coffee. Does that count?

Dr. Monroe: No, it doesn't. Coffee can make it worse. How about breakfast and lunch? What do you eat?

Tina: Uh, I don't eat. I like to sleep late, so I just grab coffee on the way to class. I basically just drink coffee all day. It keeps me _awake_ in my classes. Then I eat dinner later.

Dr. Monroe: OK, try this. I want you to drink six to eight glasses of water a day. And drink less coffee. Eat something during the day. I know you want to sleep, and it's good to sleep, but you need to eat, too.

Tina: OK, I'll try.

Dr. Monroe: I think you'll be _fine_. If your headaches don't go _away_, come back and see me again.

Part 2

Receptionist: Ramon Sanchez? You can go in.

Dr. Monroe: Hi, Ramon. What's the problem?

Ramon: I have a cold and a terrible sore _throat_.

Dr. Monroe: How about your stomach?

Ramon: No, I don't have a stomachache. It's all in my _head_.

Dr. Monroe: No cough?

Ramon: No cough.

Dr. Monroe: Well, the best thing for you to do is rest. What time do you usually go to sleep?

Ramon: Uh, about midnight or one in the morning.

Dr. Monroe: Go to bed early. You need to sleep. And drink tea and juice. Eat light foods. You can go to class, but you need to rest. A lot of students get _run_ down.

Ramon: OK, so there's no _medicine_ I can take?

Dr. Monroe: Sleep is the best thing. I think you'll feel better soon. If you don't by, say and Friday, come, see me again. Get some _rest_ now.

Ramon: OK, thanks.

BONUS QUESTION

What would you say to Tina if you were a doctor? Write the conversation.

Listen to the speakers. Write the missing words.

Self-Study CD, Track 30

Part 1

Seri: I studied in New York at Columbia University. The university is in a great _____. Riverside Park is right there. There are tons of restaurants. Some people say New York can be _____, but I felt safe there. There are so many people on the streets at almost all hours. Oh, and the transportation is great. The _____ is right there, so you can get anywhere. What else? The weather, well, the weather wasn't bad. There are four _____, and sometimes it's really beautiful, like in the spring and the fall. On Sundays I used to go to Central Park and just walk around. Any season it's a beautiful park. Oh, and there were students there from _____. I made friends with people from all over the world. It was great to go there.

Part 2

Pieter: I was in Brisbane, Australia, at the University of Queensland. Brisbane is a great place. I liked the _____. It's really _____ there. You can even walk into the stores without shoes. And there are so many great places to hang out. Gardens, _____. And the weather. Yeah, the weather is good. It's _____. Not too hot or too cold. And I always felt safe there. It was an easy place to live.

Part 3

Carla: I studied in Edinburgh, Scotland, at the university there. I'm really glad I went there. Edinburgh is a _____ city. There are so many old, wonderful _____. Of course, the weather isn't great. It's very rainy and cloudy, and sometimes really windy. But I got used to it. It's easy to get around the city. The public transportation was good, and people always _____ me, even when I got lost. What else? Oh, yeah, there's the Edinburgh International _____. It's in August. It was so fun. It was three weeks of music, and _____, and dance, and everything. People came from all over the world.

BONUS QUESTION

What do you think an exchange student would say about your hometown?
Write the conversation.

Unit 1
doing, apartment, about, hey, hope, comes, something, room, sign, see

Unit 2
rental, furnished, appliances, floors, location, reasonable, living, bathroom, antique, balcony

Unit 3
sexy, logo, skirts, sneakers, accessories, earrings, shiny, look, lipstick, perfume

Unit 4
States, American, western, visitor, guidebook, Mexican, tourist, Italy, Rome, Florence

Unit 5
person, row, thin, jeans, sleeves, Hawaiian, long, dress, baggy, red

Unit 6
household, wife, children, people, younger, parents, father, mother, home, extended, immediate, daughters

Unit 7
start, close, blocks, views, along, place, top, turn, hill, everywhere

Unit 8
bright pink, brown, green; stay home and read, go snowboarding, visit an art museum; IM your friends, go to a party, play computer games; a fluffy, white cat, a snake, a goldfish; practice yoga, go to a club with friends, go to bed; put it in the bank, have a big party, take an art class; read all of the instructions, just use it, read a few instructions; keep quiet, say something, just forget about it; get angry, call a friend to chat; relax and hang out; finish, then call her back, talk to her as long as she needs to, tell her not to worry

Unit 9
away, late, loser, now, schedule, paper, invite, back, workout, skip

Unit 10
made, around, route, work, starting, way, figure, total, done, rest

Unit 11
4.75, 5.50, 5.50, $6, $6, $10, $16, twenty

Unit 12
busy, around, nothing, relax, action, part-time, together, shopping, weekend, finish, scream, clubs

Unit 13
sauce, Greek, steps, flour, bowl, pull, ingredients, peanut, wet, mushroom, vegetables, oven

Unit 14
matter, serious, get, awake, fine, away, throat, head, run, medicine, rest

Unit 15
neighborhood, dangerous, subway, seasons, everywhere, pace, relaxed, parks, comfortable, beautiful, buildings, helped, Festival, theater

■ Coursebooks

■ Skills Books

www.impactseries.com